A MACDONALD BOOK

Text copyright © 1988 Anne Forsyth
Illustrations copyright © 1988 Toni Goffe

First published in Great Britain in 1988
by Macdonald & Co (Publishers) Ltd
London & Sydney
A Pergamon Press plc company

Photoset in 18pt Bembo by Keene Graphics Ltd, London
Colour origination by Scantrans Pte Ltd, Singapore

Printed and bound in Spain
by Cronion S.A.

Macdonald & Co (Publishers) Ltd
Greater London House
Hampstead Road
London NW1 7QX

BRITISH LIBRARY CATALOGUING IN PUBLICATION DATA
Forsyth, Anne, 1933-
The digger.
I. Title II. Goffe, Toni
823'.914[J]

ISBN 0-356-16048-3
ISBN 0-356-16049-1 Pbk

Anne Forsyth

The Digger

Illustrated by Toni Goffe

Macdonald

Chapter One

"They're at it again!" said Daniel's dad.

For weeks the men had been digging at the end of the road.

"First it was the gas, and then the water, and now it's the council."

Daniel liked to watch the workmen. "I wouldn't mind digging holes in the road, and sitting in a little hut, and making tea over a fire," he said.

But one morning he went along the road to school and there was no one there. No workmen. No one brewing tea. No one digging. Just a hole in the road.

Daniel looked at the hole and wondered how deep it was. Perhaps it went down, down, down into the ground.

"Hallo there!" said a voice. Daniel looked round, surprised. But there was no one there.

"I'm over here," said the voice.

Daniel could hardly believe his eyes. There, sitting on the edge of the pavement, was a kangaroo.

"Take a good look," said the kangaroo. "You don't see many of us around here."

A real kangaroo! A talking kangaroo! Daniel just stared.

Then he said, "But...but, where have you come from?"

"Australia," said the kangaroo in an off-hand way, as if kangaroos arrived in Laburnum Avenue every day of the week.

"I know!" said Daniel. "You've come from a zoo."

"No, I haven't," said the kangaroo a little crossly. "I told you. I've come all the way from Australia. I came up that hole," and it nodded towards the hole in the road.

The kangaroo yawned. "It was a very long journey." It jumped about for a little. "That's better. I was quite stiff. Now who are you?"

"I'm Daniel – I live at number ten Laburnum Avenue. It's just along the road."

The kangaroo held out a paw. "Hallo there, Daniel."

Daniel backed away. He couldn't wait to get to his friend Mike's house – just a few doors away.

"Wait there!" he said. "I'll be back in a moment."

Wouldn't Mike be amazed!

"A – what?" said Mike's mum.

"A talking kangaroo! Well, that's a good one!" laughed Mike's dad.

"Hurry!" said Mike. "Must see it."

They rushed back along the road, but when they got to the hole, the kangaroo had vanished.

"It *was* here," said Daniel.

"I don't believe it. You're making it up," said Mike very crossly and he wouldn't speak to Daniel all the way to school.

Chapter Two

At school that day they were talking about strange wild animals.

Daniel stood up. Surely someone would believe him.

"I saw a kangaroo," he said.

"Good!" said the teacher.

"Now where was that – at the zoo, or in a book?"

"In our road," said Daniel. "It came up a hole all the way from Australia."

Everyone laughed like anything and one boy nearly fell off his seat.

"That's enough," said the teacher. "Don't be silly, Daniel."

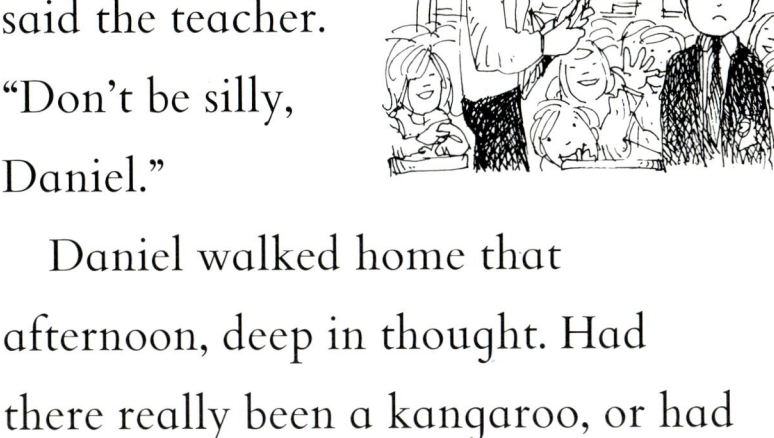

Daniel walked home that afternoon, deep in thought. Had there really been a kangaroo, or had he imagined it?

"I bet they didn't believe you," said a voice.

Daniel turned round. There, looking out of the hole in the road, was the kangaroo. It gave a great jump and landed right beside Daniel.

"No," said Daniel, "they didn't believe me."

"Hard luck," said the kangaroo. "Well, here I am. Listen, could you get me some food?"

"I suppose so," said Daniel. "But I don't know what kangaroos eat."

"Anything will do," said the kangaroo. "I'm not fussy. I'm very very hungry."

"I'll see what I can find," said Daniel. "Wait here."

So he rushed home. He opened the fridge, then looked in the kitchen cupboards.

From the fridge he took half a steak pie.

From the cupboard he took a packet of cereal.

And he took three bananas and some apples from the fruit bowl.

Surely that would be enough.

He put all the food into his school bag and went off back to the hole in the road.

The kangaroo was waiting for him. "What have you got?"

"There's cereal and steak pie and apples and bananas," said Daniel.

"That'll do," said the kangaroo, cramming bananas into its mouth.

Daniel did think that the kangaroo might have said 'thank you'. After all, he had gone to a lot of trouble.

He watched as the kangaroo scoffed the lot.

"Good on you, cobber," it said with its mouth full. Then, with a wave, it disappeared down the hole. "Be seeing you."

"Hey, wait," said Daniel, but the kangaroo had gone.

Chapter Three

Daniel's mum was very puzzled when she found the pie was missing.

"There was nearly a whole steak pie," she said. "Daniel, have you eaten it?"

"No," said Daniel which was quite true, because he hadn't eaten it, not himself anyway.

"You didn't give it to the dog, did you?"

Daniel shook his head. "No, I didn't."

Snuffy, the family mongrel, sat with his head on one side, the way he always did when people spoke about food.

"And I bought a pound of eating apples," Mum went on. "And there were three bananas left in the fruit bowl. Someone's eaten the lot."

"It wasn't me," said Daniel's big sister.

"And *I* didn't eat them," said Daniel in a very small voice.

Next morning, Daniel's big sister said, "There's no cereal left."

"Don't be silly," said Mum. "I bought a new packet yesterday."

"Well, it's not there," said Daniel's big sister.

Mum groaned. "Things just vanish in this house. I don't know how it happens."

Daniel wondered what Mum would say if he confessed that he took the pie and apples and bananas and cereal and gave them to a kangaroo. Perhaps it was better just to keep quiet about it.

But he did hope he'd see the kangaroo again.

There were so many things he wanted to ask. How long did it take to get from Australia? Who dug the tunnel to begin with? And did it join in the middle?

Next morning he left for school very early.

"Hi there, sport!" said a voice.

The kangaroo was looking over the edge of the hole.

"Hallo!" said Daniel, pleased to see that the kangaroo was real after all.

"Tell you something," said the kangaroo, "I'm a bit cold. I don't suppose you could bring me something warm to wear?"

Daniel thought for a moment. "I've a jersey. I'll bring it along after school."

"That'll do," said the kangaroo, and it disappeared down the hole again.

"Hey, stop!" called Daniel. "I wanted to ask you about the tunnel."

But the kangaroo had gone.

Chapter Four

That day at school, Daniel was careful to say nothing about the kangaroo. Everyone would think he was making it up. There were all sorts of people walking about early in the morning – the postman, the milkman, the lollipop lady.

But no one else seemed to have noticed the kangaroo.

In the afternoon, when he got back from school, Daniel hunted through his clothes. He found the bright-red and white striped jersey that Grandma had given him. Just the thing! It was much too big. The sleeves were far too long and it hung down nearly to his knees. It was sure to fit the kangaroo.

"Not bad, eh?" said the kangaroo, who didn't seem to have heard of 'please' or 'thank you' or 'good of you to take the trouble' – the kind of thing that Daniel's mum was always on about. "This'll do."

The jersey was just right for the kangaroo, and in fact it looked quite smart in it.

"I wanted to ask you," said Daniel, "about the tunnel, and getting to Australia. If I went down the tunnel..."

But the kangaroo had vanished, down the hole again.

Daniel was quite cross. He called and called but there was no reply.

It was a pity that Grandma arrived that very afternoon.

"Hallo, Daniel," she said, delving into her bag and bringing out surprises, the way she always did when she came to visit. Maybe a book or a comic or a bag of sweets.

"Oh, Daniel," she said, "that jersey I bought you – they said they'd change it. Silly of me to buy the wrong size but there's no harm done."

Daniel gulped. "It's all right, Grandma, really," he said. "I don't mind it big."

"Don't be silly, Daniel," said Mum. "Off you go and fetch it."

Daniel went upstairs very very slowly. How was he going to get out of this? He couldn't say the moths had eaten it. Not a whole jersey. He couldn't say he had left it at school, because he hadn't worn it yet. This time, he'd just have to tell the truth.

"I'm sorry, Grandma," he said, "I gave it to a kangaroo who was feeling the cold."

"Daniel, don't be so naughty and difficult." Mum was very cross indeed. "Making up silly stories like that. Grandma's been very kind to you – you don't deserve to have anything else bought for you."

Daniel was really upset. He was very fond of Grandma and felt sure she would have understood about the kangaroo.

Chapter Five

Next morning, there was still a hole in the road. Daniel tried to hurry past.

"Yoo-hoo," said a voice.

Daniel turned round. "You got me into a lot of trouble," he told the kangaroo.

It was sitting on the edge of the hole wearing the red and white striped jersey.

"A-tishoo," said the kangaroo. "I've got a code in by dose."

Certainly the kangaroo did look miserable and Daniel felt sorry for it.

"I don't subbose," said the kangaroo, "you could find me a blanket and a hot water bottle and a few paper hankies and maybe some cough sweets?"

"Oh, all right," said Daniel, because he was very kind and didn't like to see the kangaroo looking so miserable.

So he went home from school that afternoon and collected a box of paper handkerchiefs, a box of throat sweets, a hot water bottle and a blanket off his bed. Then he went back along the road.

"A-tishoo," said a voice, and the kangaroo popped its head out of the hole. "It's this awful weather. It seems to rain all the time here. No wonder I've got a cold."

Daniel gave the kangaroo the hankies and throat sweets and the hot water bottle and the blanket.

"Brrr," said the kangaroo. "I'm still shivering... what I need is a nice warm woolly scarf to put round my neck."

"Oh, all right," said Daniel, and he unwound his school scarf from his neck and gave it to the kangaroo.

"That's better," said the kangaroo, winding it round its own neck.

"Now," said Daniel, "about Australia – could I get there, if I went down the hole?"

But the kangaroo just sneezed.
"Sorry, got to go."

Daniel was really cross by now. "I've helped you a lot," he said, "and you aren't a bit grateful. You won't answer a simple question."

But the kangaroo didn't hear him. It had vanished down the hole. Daniel peered down into the hole but he couldn't see anything. And all he could hear was a distant sound – "A-tishoo..."

Chapter Six

Of course there was trouble about the missing tissues and throat sweets. And even more trouble when Mum found out that there was a blanket and a hot water bottle and Daniel's new school scarf missing.

"You won't get any more pocket money until the scarf is paid for," she said.

Daniel was really mad. It was all the kangaroo's fault. He certainly wasn't going to help the kangaroo again – he had made up his mind.

He decided he would walk along the road with his head in the air. It could sneeze all it liked and pretend it was cold and hungry and he wouldn't take a bit of notice.

So he marched past the hole in the road with his head in the air, waiting for the voice calling, "Hallo, sport!"

But there was no sound. Slowly he turned his head. There was no kangaroo, no hole in the road. The little hut had gone, and the road was as smooth and flat as it had been all those weeks ago.

Daniel didn't mention the kangaroo's disappearance - not to Mum and Dad, nor his sister, nor Grandma, nor his friends - because no one had believed him to begin with. He could hardly believe it himself. And yet - his scarf, the blanket and jersey and all the other things were missing.

One morning, a few months later, Mum collected the post from the doormat.

"Oh, look," she said, "it's a postcard – from Australia. But we don't know anyone in Australia. Oh, it's for you – Daniel."

Daniel took the card. On the front was a picture of a smiling kangaroo. On the back were Daniel's name and address – but nothing else, except a large, muddy paw print.

"That's a real puzzle," said Mum. "Who could have sent it?"

Daniel didn't say anything at all. Because he *knew*.